101 ESSENTIAL LISTS
FOR USING ICT
IN THE CLASSROOM

George Cole

continuum
LONDON • NEW YORK

Continuum International Publishing Group
The Tower Building   80 Maiden Lane
11 York Road   Suite 704
London   New York
SE1 7NX   NY 10038

www.continuumbooks.com

British Library Cataloguing-in-Publication Data
A catalogue record for this book is available from the British Library.

ISBN: 0-8264-8869-2 (paperback)

Library of Congress Cataloging-in-Publication Data
A Catalog record for this book is available from the Library of Congress

Typeset by YHT Ltd
Printed and bound in Great Britain by Ashford Colour Press Ltd,
Gosport, Hampshire

CONTENTS

The Basics 1

Why we use ICT in schools

We are living in a modern world, where even the most straightforward job may involve the use of a computer. It's vital, therefore, that children leave schools equipped with the basic ICT skills. In schools, ICT can be used to:

- help raise standards in areas such as literacy and numeracy
- offer ways of communicating, including email, instant messaging, chat and video conferencing. These can span time and distance and cost next to nothing to use
- help foster creativity, with lots of tools such as word processors, graphics packages, music creation packages and digital video programs
- enable students to review and revise their work, e.g. a word processor makes it easy to add or delete text, as well as cut-and-paste
- strengthen home–school links through email, school websites and intranets.
- motivate by putting the child in control of his or her learning, offering a variety of new and interesting tasks and presenting information in more stimulating ways
- raise self-esteem, e.g. a child with poor handwriting can produce neatly presented work on a word processor
- help with inclusion. There are many tools to help students with special educational needs, such as text-to-speech programs for visually impaired students
- personalize learning by offering students content, resources, and teaching and learning strategies that are tailored for their individual needs
- bring a topic or subject to life using multimedia in the form of sound, video and images
- encourage collaborative working, such as small groups working on a video project or pupils from different schools working together on a project.

Management benefits

ICT doesn't just help the pupils in school – there are many good ways of using it to improve school management and administration.

○ Greater efficiency throughout the school, thanks to better communication.

○ Reporting to bodies such as local education authorities (LEAs) involves less paperwork and a reduction in associated tasks, such as filing and photocopying.

○ Records are more accurate and of a higher quality.

○ Teachers can share resources, expertise and advice.

○ Less duplication and effort when preparing lesson plans, worksheets and reports.

○ Quicker and easier communication through networking, and an increase in the potential for more non-contact time for teachers.

○ Electronic registration systems mean less paperwork and provide a quick way of determining whether a student is absent or not.

○ Teachers perform administrative tasks more quickly and with a greater degree of sophistication, e.g. when analysing students' progress and setting attainment targets.

○ Opportunities for more social contact and support among teachers.

LIST 3   Using ICT in the classroom

ICT can aid pupils' learning in the classroom (and beyond) because it:

○ is highly interactive – students can connect with learning materials in ways that are just not possible with other media, such as books or television

○ provides instant feedback, such as immediately displaying the answer to a question or showing the result of altering a variable in a simulation exercise

○ promotes higher-level thinking by removing the need to spend lots of time on lower-order tasks. For example, students don't need to collect data and then spend most of the lesson simply drawing a graph or table

○ can be used almost anywhere around a school or in the wider community, with the availability of laptops, handheld PCs and tablet PCs

○ is great for creativity, using tools like paint programs, digital cameras, music packages and word processors

○ lets you go beyond the real world and use simulation packages to explore, for example, the nucleus of an atom or the effect of gravity on the moon.

LIST 4   Basic ICT skills

Students and teachers need to have a number of basic ICT skills in order to get the most out of the technology. Here are some of them.

- Be able to switch on a computer
- Be able to switch off a computer properly
- Use a mouse to operate the PC
- Use a keyboard
- Save data
- Back up data
- Open a file
- Delete files
- Drag and drop files so they can be moved from one place to another
- Write with a word processor
- Use a database
- Use a spreadsheet
- Use the clipboard to transfer files or documents from one folder to another
- Print a document or file
- Create a basic multimedia presentation
- Launch a web browser and search the Internet
- Know how to use a search engine
- Send and receive emails
- Touch-type – although you can use a computer keyboard without being able to touch-type, having this skill is a great asset.

L I S T 5 Computer jargon

The computer world is plagued by what are known as TLAs – three-letter acronyms. Here are some of the most common ones.

○ Bit (binary digit) – the smallest amount of data used in computing. A bit is either a one or a zero.
○ Blog – short for web log, an online diary.
○ CD-ROM (compact disc read-only memory) – a CD that stores data.
○ CPU (central processing unit) – the microprocessor chip that controls the computer's operations.
○ DVD-ROM (digital versatile disc read-only memory) – a CD-sized disc that can store lots of data.
○ GB (gigabyte) – a unit of measurement for data storage that is equivalent to 1,000 megabytes. It's commonly used to denote the size of a hard-disk drive.
○ HTML (hyper text mark-up language) – the programming language used to create websites and web pages.
○ MB (megabyte) – a unit of measurement for file size or data storage.
○ Mbps (megabits per second) – a unit for measuring the speed of a data connection that is equivalent to one million bits of data per second.
○ MP3 (moving picture experts group audio layer 3) – a music file format.
○ Os (open source) – software programs and applications that are freely available for users to modify and adapt.
○ OS (operating system) – the software that controls and manages the computer's operations.
○ RAM (random access memory) – the temporary computer store which holds the programs that are currently running on a PC.
○ ROM (read-only memory) – memory that cannot be changed.
○ URL (universal resource locator) – the unique web address of a website or page.
○ WWW (World Wide Web) – the part of the Internet that contains many millions of linked websites and pages.
○ WYSIWYG (what you see is what you get) – pronounced 'wiziwig', it describes how the display you see on your computer screen is what you'll get if you print it out.

LIST 6 Email language

Most of us are used to the numerous acronyms you get in text messages (such as C U L8R for 'see you later' and B4 2nite for 'before tonight'). There are also loads of them used in email messages, designed to cut down on typing and the length of the email!

B4N – Bye for now
BRB – Be right back
BTW – By the way
CMIIW – Correct me if I'm wrong
FAQ – Frequently asked questions
G2G – Got to go
IMHO – In my humble opinion
IOW – In other words
LION – Like it or not
LOL – Laughed (or laughing) out loud
N1 – Nice one
NOYB – None of your business
PAW – Parents are watching
RTFM – Read the flipping manual (ruder alternatives are also used)
TAW – Teacher is watching
TIA – Thanks in advance
TNG – That's not good
URYYFM – You are too wise for me
WOMBAT – Waste of money, brains and time.

Using Software 2

LIST 7   Types of software

There is a wealth of software on the Internet, but not all software is the same and this is important if you are planning to download and use some.

○ Freeware – software that is freely available. However, there are often conditions attached to its use, such as for non-commercial use only.

○ Shareware – not the same as freeware, but software you can download and try before buying. Normally, users are given a fixed period in which to use the software (such as 30 days) or can only use it a limited number of times. If you decide to buy it, these restrictions are lifted.

○ Commercial software – software you buy. If you go along this route, check that you get adequate documentation and support.

○ Open source – so called because end-users are free to modify or adapt the software. Open source software is either free or much cheaper than commercial software.

LIST 8 — Popular software used in schools

Here are some examples of the type of software you are likely to encounter in the classroom.

- Word processor – many word processors are sophisticated and can be used to create a wide range of document types.
- Spreadsheet – used for various data-handling tasks.
- Database – used for organizing and sorting data.
- Desktop publishing package (DTP) – used to create all kinds of documents, from class newspapers to leaflets and posters.
- Presentation software – used to create presentations, which can contain a mix of media, such as text, graphics and sound.
- Paint program – used for drawing and painting on a computer.
- Digital editing program – used for editing and manipulating video and sound.
- Web page creation program – anyone can publish work on the Internet with this type of program.
- Drill-and-practice software – used for developing specific skills, such as learning a language.
- Problem-solving software – often found in subjects such as mathematics and science.
- Simulation software – uses graphics and animation to explain or describe a concept or phenomenon. This is a great way of helping students' understanding.
- Reference software – includes multimedia encyclopaedias and electronic dictionaries.
- Games – both educational and fun!

LIST 9   Software media

Software comes in various forms.

○ Floppy disk – mainly restricted to older software with simple text and graphics. However, just because software is old and basic doesn't mean it isn't useful!

○ CD-ROM – most software is found on this. CD-ROMs offer multimedia software with sound, video, text, graphics and animation. Despite the hype, they are not indestructible and need good care and attention. Encourage pupils to put them in their cases when not in use.

○ DVD-ROM – the same size as a CD-ROM but with a much bigger capacity (at least seven times). However, very little software is on DVD-ROM, with most software developers preferring to use multiple CD-ROMs.

○ Networked – here software is stored on a server and distributed over the network. This could be from the school's internal network or from the Internet.

How to assess software

Getting the right software for your students is the key to the successful use of ICT in the classroom. If software is boring or difficult to use, then students will gain little from it. That's why it's important that all software is carefully assessed before use.

○ Don't go on price. Just because it's free doesn't mean it's bad, and remember that expensive software can be poor!

○ Don't be dazzled by lots of multimedia. In some cases it can be merely a distraction from the poor-quality content. Some of the best programs have little or no multimedia.

○ How compatible is it with your existing ICT?

○ Age – is it relevant for your age group?

○ Ability – does it cater for the ability range?

○ Content – does it actually help to develop the relevant skills, knowledge or understanding?

○ Relevance – how relevant is it to the curriculum?

○ Flexibility – can you adapt the software for different ability levels?

○ Versatility – can you use the program for a variety of teaching and learning situations?

○ Display – are the screens clear and uncluttered?

○ Usability – how easy is it to use? Will most students be able to use it after little training?

○ How motivating is it – will users soon get bored? Does it offer instant feedback? Is there a variety of tasks to carry out?

○ Teacher controls – can you set up the program for specific tasks? Is there a system for recording student performance?

○ Accessibility – can it be used by children with special needs? For example, can you use it with a switch or touch screen?

○ Documentation – do you get a good teachers' guide? Are there worksheets or printouts?

○ Technical support – is there telephone or email support and if so, what hours is it available and how much does it cost?

The Hardware

LIST 11 Computers in schools

- Desktop computer – the workhorse of ICT in schools that can be used for many activities.
- Laptop computer – a portable computer that varies in size.
- Sub-notebook – a miniature version of a laptop, with fewer features, but ideal for carrying around.
- All-in-one – a combined monitor and desktop computer designed for saving space.
- Tablet PC – uses a pen or stylus as the main user interface. Ideal for collecting data on the move.
- Media PC – specially designed for playing back sound, music, video, DVDs, games and television.
- Thin client – also known as network computers because they are used on high-speed networks, with servers (see below) storing the programmes and doing most of the processing.
- Handheld computer – sometimes called a palmtop or PDA, these miniature machines are ideal for data collection.
- Computer desk – contains a built-in desktop computer that can be packed away when not in use.
- Word processor – a dedicated word-processor package consisting of a small screen and keyboard.
- Server – not often seen in a classroom, this is a computer that stores many files and data which are passed on to other computers on a network.
- Web cache – a computer that stores content from websites.

L I S T 12 Connecting ports on computers

The back of a computer can look a little bewildering, and even a little daunting, because of the variety of connecting ports on display. The different ports have a variety of uses and all use special connecting leads or cables.

○ USB – a high-speed plug-and-play port used by all modern computers. The first version, USB 1.1 has been superseded by a faster version, USB 2.0. Used for connecting optical mice, printers, digital cameras, portable storage devices, scanners and much more.

○ IEEE 1394 – also known as Firewire. A high-speed digital connection often used for transferring video from a digital camcorder to a computer.

○ RJ11 – for connecting a telephone modem.

○ PS/2 – for connecting a mouse and keyboard to a PC.

○ Ethernet port – for networking.

○ Headphone socket – for private listening on a computer.

○ Microphone socket – for recording audio on a computer.

○ Audio out – for sending sound to external speakers.

○ TV out – for displaying information on an external monitor.

○ S-Video – a high-quality video output socket.

○ Parallel port – an old-style connection for printers, now replaced by USB.

○ Serial port – an old-style port for mice, keyboards, digital cameras, etc., now replaced by USB.

○ SCSI – an old-style port used by Apple Macintosh computers.

L I S T 13 Looking after your computer

○ Keep it as clean and as dust-free as possible.

○ Avoid eating or drinking around your computer, as crumbs of food can make the keyboard messy and drinks can get spilt. Liquids and electricity do not mix!

○ Avoid submitting your computer to physical shocks.

○ Make sure that your computer has an anti-virus package and that it's kept up to date!

○ If you're using a computer online, make sure that there is firewall protection. Also install anti-spyware software (see List 32 Computer nasties).

○ Close all programs before shutting down your computer.

○ Always go through the proper shut-down procedure rather than simply switching the power off. Failure to do so could mean losing or corrupting data.

○ If you install a program that causes your computer to crash or become sluggish, you can use the 'system restore' feature on a Windows PC, which lets you 'wind back' your computer to a previous point before the trouble started.

○ Always go through the proper procedure for removing peripheral devices from your computer or you could damage or lose data stored on the device.

○ If your computer crashes or freezes, don't panic and simply switch off the power. There are a number of procedures which can safely shut down the computer (such as using the control-alt-delete keys on a PC to shut down the program that has crashed).

○ Always keep any supplied disks and documentation in a safe space – you never know when you'll need it!

○ Avoid touching the screen on your laptop computer.

○ Carry your laptop in a protective bag, but try and avoid ones with the manufacturer's logo – they're a temptation to thieves!

○ If your laptop contains sensitive data, you should password-protect your computer and better still, encrypt (scramble) the data.

Computer maintenance

External

○ Switch off your computer and unplug it from the mains.

○ Use a cleaning cloth, anti-static wipes or a can of compressed air.

○ Clean the monitor, keyboard, mouse (if a rollerball type) and case, using compressed air to get between the crevices.

○ Plug and unplug the connections and gently wipe the contacts if they are grubby.

○ Don't switch on again until the computer is completely dry.

Internal

○ Use the add/remove programs to get rid of unused programs.

○ Discard any unwanted files to the recycle bin and then empty it.

○ Delete temporary Internet files in the web browser.

○ Use the disk cleaner utility on Windows to remove redundant files.

○ Use the defragmenter to re-organize your hard drive.

○ Update anti-virus progams and then scan for viruses.

○ Update anti-spyware program(s) and then scan for spyware (see List 32 Computer nasties).

Health and safety issues

- Learning to touch-type not only makes it faster to type, but can help prevent repetitive strain injuries (RSI) in the wrists and hands, often caused by unorthodox typing.
- Your seat should provide good back support and be height adjustable.
- Correct posture will help to avoid back strain.
- The monitor should be adjustable for angle and tilt, with the monitor set slightly below eye level. It should also be possible to adjust brightness and contrast.
- Prevent screen glare from windows or light sources by using blinds and other types of light shields.
- The mouse should be operated with a straight wrist – use a wrist rest to reduce the risk of RSI.
- Have regular breaks to reduce the risk of eye strain, backache and RSI.
- Using an alternative keyboard can mean less stress on the hands and wrist.
- Don't look directly into the light from an interactive whiteboard projector or a data projector.
- Be careful when lifting large objects, such as old, heavy computer monitors. Some laptops can be heavy too!
- ICT equipment can generate a lot of heat, so make sure your ICT suite is well ventilated.

Why it won't work!

Computers are temperamental beasts and often go wrong at the time when you or your students are doing something important. Fortunately, many problems are easy to solve. It's also worth stressing the importance of regularly backing up and saving work as you go along, so that when the computer is fixed again, you can pick up where you left off. Common problems you will doubtless encounter include:

- no power
- no cable
- loose cable
- monitor not switched on
- new software installed which conflicts with the computer
- new hardware installed which conflicts with the computer
- component failure
- power surge damaged the computer
- network failure
- virus
- finger trouble – pressing the wrong key.

Useful peripherals

Peripherals are add-ons for your computer and some are more useful than others! The great thing about peripherals is that they extend the functionality of a computer, allowing you, for example, to print out hard-copy documents, import images or create a large screen display that can be seen by all the class at once. Most peripherals are connected to a PC via a USB port.

- Printer – for making hard copies.
- Digital camera – for taking images which can be put into a PC and edited, manipulated, posted on the Internet, emailed or placed into documents.
- Scanner – for putting printed text, pictures and graphics into a computer.
- Webcam – for communicating with others over the Internet.
- Speakers – for sound and music.
- Optical disc writer – for large back-ups and storing documents, files and data.
- USB storage device – for storing text and images in a highly portable device.
- Back-up device – for protecting valuable data and files.
- Interactive whiteboard – for teaching and class presentations.
- Data projector – for teaching and class presentations (cheaper than interactive whiteboards).
- Sensors – for data monitoring.
- Roamers – for simple programming work.
- Visualizers – for displaying 3D objects.

LIST 18   Back-up media

- Floppy disk – holds about one megabyte of data. Useful for text documents and small image files, but no good for high-resolution images, video or music.
- CD-R/RW – blank CDs that store around 700MB of data. They can store lots of text, graphics and digital images. CD-RW discs can be used and re-used like floppy disks.
- USB thumb drive – typically stores between 512MB and 1GB of data. They are very tiny, but offer similar or better storage capacity than blank CDs.
- Memory card – can typically store up to 1GB, but are expensive.
- DVD-R/RW – typically stores 4.7GB to 8.5GB. Lots of space for digital images and video.
- External hard drive – may store hundreds of gigabytes and so is ideal for backing up most if not all of your hard drive.
- Tape – can store hundreds of gigabytes of data but takes much longer to locate items than those stored on a disk.

LIST 19 Checklist: ICT inside the classroom

○ Make sure that all the equipment is in working order before the lesson starts.

○ Make sure that you have sufficient equipment for the number of pupils in the lesson.

○ Test to see if the software is installed and working.

○ Be ready with an action plan should the hardware fail – including the whole school network going down!

○ Draw up a list of skills pupils will need for the lesson, such as using a mouse, connecting a sensor to a computer, and make sure all pupils have them.

○ Set clear, focused tasks so that it is less likely that pupils will be distracted or bored and start playing with the equipment.

○ Make sure that any bags and coats are stored well away from the work areas.

○ If you're planning to use the Internet, consider downloading the content before the lesson and storing it on a web cache, if your school has one.

○ Remember, the best lessons use a mix of computer-based tasks and off-computer tasks – don't use ICT for the sake of it.

○ Make sure that every pupil gets a fair turn and that no one hogs the computer!

○ Make sure that pupils save and back up their work at the end of the lesson.

○ Check to see that pupils have closed down programs or shut down their computers properly at the end of the lesson.

LIST 20 Checklist: ICT outside the classroom

○ Count the number of computers and/or other pieces of hardware before you leave the classroom.

○ Make selected pupils responsible for their return.

○ Test to see if the relevant software is loaded and working.

○ Make sure that any peripherals, such as data loggers, are working when connected to the computer.

○ Take the appropriate number of connecting cables, adapters, etc.

○ Charge any batteries.

○ Ensure that pupils know how to use the equipment and how to take care of it.

○ Try and take some spare hardware in case of damage or breakdown.

○ Make sure that pupils can also do some work on paper in case their equipment fails.

○ Stress the importance of safely storing any collected data.

○ Count the pieces of hardware before you leave the locality.

○ Count the equipment again back in the classroom.

○ If possible, transfer any recorded or collected data to a desktop PC or storage device before the lesson ends.

○ Recharge batteries if required.

Preparing for digital video

Digital video can bring a subject to life by recording moving pictures and sound. Students can also become active participants in their learning, rather than just passively watching a video. Pupils also use a large variety of skills with digital video, including scripting, recording, directing, editing and collaborating (see List 75 Why use digital video in the classroom?). Some of the hardware you might need for this includes:

- a digital camcorder
- a Firewire cable for connecting the camcorder to the PC and transferring footage
- a computer with a fast processor, lots of RAM memory and lots of hard-disk space
- an external hard drive for storing video footage – video files are massive and use up lots of hard-disk capacity
- headphones for monitoring sound
- a microphone for dubbing sound effects or adding narration
- a DVD burner for putting your video footage on to disc – these will play on most DVD players and drives.

Twelve ways to use sensors

Everyday life is full of interesting physical phenomena, from fast-changing temperatures to slow-growing plants. Sensors and data-monitoring software and hardware can be used for recording events that happen very quickly or over a long period of time. Here are a few ideas for things you could measure.

1 Heart rate – during physical activity.
2 Temperature – both inside and outside the classroom.
3 Conductivity – useful for various electrical experiments.
4 Current – great for physics lessons.
5 Humidity – in a classroom or greenhouse.
6 pH – useful for biology and chemistry.
7 Speed of sound – physics students can have fun with this one!
8 Infra-red light – useful for detecting heat.
9 Force – lots of applications in physics lessons.
10 Voltage – useful for physics lessons.
11 Oxygen level – in biology or PE lessons.
12 Motion – use this in PE when students are running or jogging.

LIST 23 Ten good reasons to use a tablet PC

Tablet PCs are not like ordinary PCs. For a start, users can input data with their normal handwriting, as tablet PCs use handwriting recognition software. This makes a tablet PC ideal for children with poor typing skills or for times when it's easier to write than type, such as ticking off a list. There are a lot of benefits to both teachers and students in using a tablet PC.

1 It uses an electronic stylus or pen interface, rather than a keyboard or mouse.
2 It is highly portable.
3 Users can make written notes and convert them to electronic text.
4 Pupils can email assignments to the teacher, who can make written annotations and email them back.
5 Chemical equations can be put into a computer without the need for special software.
6 It is ideal for collecting data around the school or on a field trip.
7 Internet access is available via either a wired or wireless network connection.
8 There is a growing range of software packages specially developed for tablet PCs.
9 It can be used for student registration.
10 It can be used as a portable presentation tool with a data projector.

Mobile phone possibilities

Many pupils already carry a pocket PC – their mobile phone. Like an ordinary computer, mobile phones have a processor chip and computer memory and can store data. Many also have web browsers too, and can even be linked to a PC (via a USB cable, Bluetooth or infra-red wireless connection or memory card) for transferring data or images. With a suitably equipped mobile phone pupils can do many things, such as:

○ take digital still images which can then be emailed to other people
○ record video clips and email them
○ record sound
○ record data
○ access the Internet via the phone's web browser
○ use email
○ download files, such as educational games, from the Internet
○ watch streaming media, such as video
○ read electronic books
○ use personal digital assistant-like features, such as a calendar and to-do list
○ use cut-down versions of *Word* and *Excel*
○ use a Bluetooth wireless connection to communicate with a laptop.

LIST 25   Going wireless

Wireless computing means no more wires, no more cables and no more being tied to a desktop. Many computer devices can operate wirelessly, including, desktop PCs, laptops, tablet PCs, data projectors, mice and keyboards.

There are two basic types of wireless technology: Bluetooth, a short-range system that is designed to replace cables, and 802.11 (better known as WiFi), a standard for wireless networks. More and more schools are opting for wireless networking because of the benefits it offers:

- ○ Freedom and flexibility to use ICT away from the desktop and indeed, away from the classroom, while still in touch with the school network. A PE teacher, for example, could use a laptop with a wireless link on the sports field.
- ○ Wireless computing is becoming easier, cheaper and faster.
- ○ More and more ICT products and devices have wireless networking built in as standard.
- ○ There's no need to drill holes in walls and run cables all over the place to create your network.
- ○ Wireless networking offers quick way of extending the reach of a wired network, for example, to a temporary classroom.

LIST 26   Wireless networking: the downside

Of course, there is a downside to most things, and before you plunge into wireless networking, you should be aware of the potential problems.

- ❍ It can be tricky to set up, especially when mixing and matching products from different manufacturers.
- ❍ It's less secure than a wired network.
- ❍ Data speeds are slower than those possible with a wired network.
- ❍ It is not suitable for streaming large multimedia files.
- ❍ It can suffer interference from microwaves and cordless phones.
- ❍ Signals can be blocked by some building materials.
- ❍ Wireless blackspots, where the signal can't reach, are not uncommon.
- ❍ The operating distance is rarely as long as it says on the box.
- ❍ Despite Bluetooth being an agreed standard, some Bluetooth devices will not communicate with other Bluetooth devices.

What to do when things go wrong

Three things are inevitable in life – death, taxes and that ICT will let you down at some stage. To combine two well-known sayings – don't panic and be prepared. Here are some steps you can take when things don't go according to plan:

○ Wherever possible, plan ahead to reduce the impact of failure. For example, if possible have spare equipment available, use a web cache to store web pages so they are available if the Internet connection falls down, and have the ICT technician to hand.

○ Get trained in the basic techniques for sorting out common problems, such as re-booting when the computer crashes, closing down a program that isn't working properly, checking a plug fuse and making sure any connections are correct and firmly in place.

○ If a single computer fails, re-organize groups so that additional members can join them, or have some additional non-computer tasks to hand, for example, written work or using a camcorder.

○ If the whole network goes down, have additional resources to hand. These might include:
  – printouts and worksheets
  – a blackboard or whiteboard for whole-group presentations
  – books
  – alternative audio and video sources, such as videos, DVDs and audio recorders.

○ Use the opportunity to show how important computers are in teaching and learning these days. For example, if the group was using ICT to collect data or create a graph, get the pupils to do this by using a pencil and paper and then ask them to write about the difference.

Home truths

○ If anything can go wrong, it probably already has.
○ Computers always work perfectly until the pupils arrive.
○ You always wish you had one more computer in the classroom.
○ You can never find a technician when you need one.
○ Pupils will almost invariably know more about computers than you.
○ You can never find the right connecting cable when you need it.
○ Computers are like humans, very temperamental – only more so.
○ The computer always crashes at the one time when you forget to back up your data.
○ Whatever computer you buy today, the one on sale tomorrow will be smaller, smarter, faster – and cheaper.
○ You'll never know everything there is to know about computers.

Keeping ICT Safe and Secure

LIST 29   Good password practice

Passwords are used to restrict access and protect data. In most schools, teachers will have individual passwords and in many, pupils have their own password to log on to the school network.

- Choose a password with at least six characters.
- Never choose passwords that are easy to crack, such as your name, your date of birth or words like 'password'.
- The best passwords use a mix of letters and numbers.
- Try and use passwords that are easy for you to remember but hard for someone to guess. For example, Jane Smith who was born on 17/10/87 and has a cat called Max might opt to use SJ17Max87.
- Never write down your password and leave it near your computer.
- Never share your password with anyone.
- Never ask the computer to remember your password automatically. It's convenient, but means anyone logging on to your machine could access your email or data.
- Be wary of 'shoulder surfers' when you're typing your password.
- If you're using a public computer, such as a machine in a library or Internet café, clear the web browser cache after use, and the web history. If you're not sure how to do this on your web browser – find out now!
- Change your password on a regular basis.

LIST 30   Safe Internet surfing in schools

The Internet is a wonderful resource for communication, content and collaboration, but it can also be a source of danger, which is why safety policies need to be developed for school use.

○ Install Internet traffic filters that can block sites, web pages or other unwanted content. But note that no filter is perfect.

○ Use a firewall to monitor and control the data traffic between the Internet and your network.

○ Use anti-virus software to scan incoming and outgoing files and emails.

○ Use monitoring systems that allow staff to see which websites and web pages have been viewed by individual pupils. Some also allow emails to be monitored. If you use monitoring technology, staff and pupils need to be made aware of it.

○ Use an Internet service provider (ISP), local educational authority or regional broadband consortium (RBC) that offers good protection, such as strong filtering or monitoring.

○ Consider using a web cache, which allows vast amounts of online content to be downloaded and stored. Schools can use a web cache as an Internet 'walled garden' but bear in mind that this limits the pupils' freedom to explore online and discover things for themselves.

Developing a school policy

All schools have a duty of care to pupils and so it's sensible to develop a policy that outlines what the school considers to be acceptable behaviour when going online. This policy should be made known to the pupils and signed ideally by both parents and teachers. It also needs to be reviewed regularly to take in new developments, such as accessing the Internet via a mobile phone. An 'acceptable use policy' might set out guidelines prohibiting:

- access to pornographic, violent, racist or anti-religious sites
- access to sport and entertainment sites, unless instructed by a teacher
- access to chat sites or forums, unless designated by a teacher
- the downloading of illegal software or media files, such as music files or video clips
- the installation of unauthorised software
- online bullying
- the sending of offensive email messages
- the sending of personal information, such as your name and address, unless a teacher has given permission
- the downloading of games and ring tones.

It might also provide guidance on:

- using webcams responsibly
- respecting copyright and not downloading material to pass off as your own work.

L I S T 32   Computer nasties

There are a variety of Internet nasties that come under the umbrella of 'malware'. They all have one thing in common – they are not good for your computer or your school network.

- ○ Viruses – rogue programs that can damage, disrupt or disable a computer or computer network. They spread from file to file.
- ○ Worms – these can also cause damage or disruption, but unlike viruses are able to self-replicate and spread.
- ○ Trojan horse – a rogue program that is hidden in another seemingly harmless program.
- ○ Spyware – a program that tracks your web browser behaviour and sends it to a third party.
- ○ Adware – annoying programs which cause unwanted banners and pop-up advertisements to appear on your computer screen.
- ○ Dialler – a program that hijacks your computer modem and causes it to ring a premium-rate number.
- ○ Browser hijacker – this takes over your browser and causes you to visit unwanted websites.
- ○ Keyboard logger – this logs every keystroke and sends information to a hacker's website. Vital information, such as passwords and bank details, can be stolen this way.
- ○ Home-page hijacker – a program which changes the home page on your browser.
- ○ Spam – unsolicited email that can clog up your mailbox.
- ○ Phishing emails – fake emails purporting to come from a legitimate source, such as an online bank, and designed to get the recipient to reveal personal information like passwords.
- ○ Spoofed emails – fake emails that use legitimate email addresses and so fool recipients into thinking the message is from a friend or acquaintance.

Internet safety and your home computer

As a teacher you will need to use the computer a lot at home. Here are some things you can do to ensure that your home computer stays trouble-free as well.

- Install an anti-virus program and keep it regularly updated.
- Install a firewall.
- Install anti-spyware programs.
- Install anti-spam software.
- If you're using a dial-up modem, you are at risk from diallers – rogue programs that connect your computer to premium-rate phone lines and run up massive bills. Run regular checks with anti-dialler software and always unplug your PC from the phone socket when you're not online.
- Never open unsolicited attachments and watch out for file names such as .exe, .pif, .scr, .vbs, as these are often used by virus writers. Also watch out for double extensions designed to disguise viruses, such as .jpeg.exe.
- Download attachments to your hard drive and then scan them with an anti-virus program before opening them.
- Install the latest version of any web browser, as this will offer stronger protection.
- Set up your computer so that any security updates are automatically downloaded to your PC.
- Consider using alternative operating systems to Microsoft Windows, such as Apple or Linux, as to date these have had far fewer viruses.
- Consider using an alternative web browser to Microsoft's Internet Explorer, such as Firefox, whose supporters say is more secure.
- Take appropriate steps to make your wireless network, if you have one, more secure. These work by sending data around on radio waves, which means an end to having your computer tethered to a telephone socket, but this freedom comes at a price. Try encrypting or scrambling data so it can't easily be seen by unauthorised persons, and 'hiding' your network – the instructions on how to do this should come with your wireless network package.
- Be vigilant – there is no such thing as total protection. You

should also regularly back up vital data and have a contingency plan ready for a time when your computer or network is infected with a virus or some other unwanted visitor.

ICT in the Classroom 5

Planning a lesson using ICT

○ Don't use ICT for the sake of it – ask yourself, is ICT the best way of achieving my teaching and learning objectives?

○ If you are not confident about using ICT, seek support from your colleagues.

○ Don't forget that many pupils are confident and competent users of ICT – they've grown up in a world of computers! Don't see this as a threat to your authority, but as an opportunity to get some extra help and support. Pupils love taking on the role of an 'expert' and it raises their self-esteem. They won't think less of you if you ask for help.

○ When planning, look for activities or events where ICT could be used.

○ Don't forget about portable computers like laptops and tablet PCs – ICT does not have to be confined to the classroom!

○ ICT is great for eliminating boring, repetitive or time-consuming tasks, such as drawing a table. Use the spare time this creates for higher-order activities.

○ Don't re-invent the wheel. Many teachers have already developed ICT content or strategies and discovered what works and what doesn't. Talk to colleagues and get online – there are lots of school websites, teacher websites and online communities where people are sharing ideas, lesson plans and experiences (see List 54 Websites for teachers). Don't forget to share some of your good ideas too!

○ The best lessons are a mix of ICT-related tasks and off-computer tasks.

○ When planning a lesson, check which ICT resources are available, including hardware, software and technical support.

○ Check any software before use and make sure it does what you want it to do.

○ Check websites for content and suitability before using them.

○ If your school has a web cache (which stores web pages) then use it for storing the important websites or web pages you are planning to use.

L I S T 35   Getting prepared

Before the pupils enter the room, it's best to have everything in place and be sure of how you want the lesson to progress. Here's a quick checklist to run through.

- ◯ Do you have all the relevant hardware, software and peripherals? Is Internet access in place?
- ◯ Do the students have the relevant skills or will you have to start off the lesson demonstrating some of them?
- ◯ Do they all have passwords for logging onto the network?
- ◯ How do you want the students to work – as a whole class watching you use a digital projector or interactive whiteboard? In small groups? Individually?
- ◯ Are the ICT tasks focused? For example, if the students are going online, do you they know which websites to visit or what to search for?
- ◯ Have you got sufficient hardware and software for the group or will some pupils have to do other tasks away from the computer until it's their turn?
- ◯ Have you given the pupils enough time to carry out the ICT tasks and other activities, such as writing a report or packing away?
- ◯ Do pupils know how to save and back up their work?
- ◯ Do you have a plan in place should the ICT fail?

LIST 36 Children with special educational needs

One of the great things about ICT is its ability to make teaching and learning more inclusive for children with special educational needs by enabling them to create, participate and collaborate in a lesson. Computers make it possible to offer a series of simple, structured tasks; they're interactive, can offer instant feedback and support, can help children who have difficulties with normal social interaction – and they are endlessly patient!

Examples of special educational needs include:

○ Dyslexia – this usually involves difficulties with writing, reading and spelling. There may also be speech, handwriting or comprehension difficulties.
○ Dyscalculia – difficulties with mathematical skills and concepts.
○ Dyspraxia – this is an umbrella term for conditions affecting motor skills. These can make it difficult or even impossible to use a keyboard or mouse.
○ Visual impairments – these can' vary from mild visual conditions to complete blindness.
○ Hearing impairments – these also vary considerably.
○ Behavioural, social or emotional problems – these can include attention deficit hyperactivity disorder (ADHD) and varying degrees of autism.

L I S T 37   Using ICT for SEN

With an estimated one in five school children having some form of special educational need (SEN), it is inevitable that you will have pupils in your classroom that need a bit of extra help. Make sure you communicate with your school's special educational needs coordinator (SENCO) as they will have detailed knowledge of the pupil's needs. However, when using ICT with these pupils there are a few basic things to remember:

- Check that the screen is adjusted correctly and at the correct height and angle for the seating.
- Ensure that any seating is comfortable for the pupil.
- Check that the workstation layout is easy for the pupil to operate.
- Provide a cordless optical mouse if possible as it is easier to use than one tethered to a computer.

Most computer operating systems have built-in accessibility features so that you are able to make adjustments to suit an individual pupil's needs. Features you will be able to adjust include:

- mouse speeds
- keyboard response times, so you don't get multiple letters when you hold down for a long timeeee
- font size and colour
- size of the icons
- screen contrast and resolution
- size of the cursor and its blinking speed
- screen magnification – making parts of the screen larger
- volume – you can have sound effects when various features are activated.
- sticky keys – make it easier to carry out commands that require two or more keys to be pressed simultaneously
- filter keys – ignore certain keystrokes.

Add-ons for SEN

As well as making basic adjustments to your school computer to help children with special educational needs (see List 37 Using ICT for SEN), there are a number of additional ways to make ICT more accessible for them.

- Mouse substitutes, such as roller balls and joysticks can help children with motor skills difficulties.
- Switches are a good replacement for a mouse.
- Touch screens are useful for children who have problems using a keyboard or mouse.
- Braille keyboards can help some visually impaired children.
- Braille labels are also useful for some visually impaired children.
- Speech synthesisers can help visually impaired children.
- Screen readers convert text to speech and can be used for reading text from a screen.
- Talking word processors can help children with reading difficulties.
- Predictive word processors make educated guesses at the word you are about to type and present an on-screen list of possible words. This is useful for slow typists and children who have problems with spelling.
- Overlay keyboards make it much simpler to operate a computer by using large touch-sensitive grids.

LIST 39 Presentations with PowerPoint

Microsoft's PowerPoint is the most common presentation software found in schools, used by both students and teachers. Here are a few tips for putting together effective presentations.

○ Forget about PowerPoint being a boring business presentation tool – it can be used to create stimulating, informative and entertaining presentations.

○ Don't fall into the B&B trap – bullet points and boring delivery. Use a variety of media – text, graphics, animations, sound and video.

○ Add web links to your presentation.

○ Make your presentation more interesting by using hyperlinks between slides, allowing you to jump from one slide to another and back.

○ Keep it simple – don't use too much text on each slide or too many bullet points – your audience won't be able to keep up with the flood of information.

○ Make text as large as possible and keep it well spaced.

○ Don't use too many fonts or choose font styles that are difficult to read.

○ Don't use too many colours as this could give your audience a headache!

○ Make sure the background colours do not clash with the text or make it difficult to read.

○ Remember, your presentation is not set in stone – it's easy to make amendments and add or remove slides.

○ Consider using your PowerPoint presentation with a data projector or interactive whiteboard.

○ Put your PowerPoint presentation on the school intranet or the Internet.

○ Get your students to prepare a storyboard before starting work on their own presentations.

○ Be imaginative – PowerPoint can be used to create animated interactive stories, quizzes, puzzles and much more!

○ Checkout these useful links:
  – PowerPoint in the Classroom – www.actden.com/pp
  – PowerPoint Answers – www.powerpointanswers.com

- PowerPoint tutorials – www.ictadvice.org.uk/ new2computers/opt/menu_pres/page/tutorials
- PowerPoint resources – www.educationusingpowerpoint.org.uk.

LIST 40   Interactive whiteboards

An interactive whiteboard is essentially a large touch-sensitive computer screen. It consists of a screen, computer and data projector (which puts the computer display on the screen). Options include:

○ touch-sensitive screens – can be operated by a finger or inkless pen (they look like ordinary felt-tip pens but are dry). The finger can be used like a computer mouse to operate the whiteboard, for example, opening up a program or closing a window. The pens allow users to 'write' and 'draw' on the board.

○ non touch-sensitive screens – can't be operated with a finger, but use special pens.

○ portable interactive whiteboards – small handheld devices that can be carried around a classroom and used almost anywhere.

○ some interactive whiteboards come with an electronic voting system. Pupils use tiny handheld devices that look a little like a simplified remote control handset to make their vote, which is displayed on the interactive whiteboard. These are great for using in debates and discussions and getting pupils to focus on an issue, for example, should junk food be banned in school canteens?

○ whiteboards can be permanently mounted (fixed) or portable. Portable whiteboards usually consist of a trolley which holds a screen and a laptop computer.

LIST 41 — Why interactive whiteboards work

Interactive whiteboards have many benefits in the classroom and are increasingly popular in schools because they:

- are great for displaying things to a large group
- can display a wide range of media, including, text, graphics, animations, video and websites
- are more versatile than a conventional blackboard or whiteboard
- support collaborative learning – pupils can share ideas easily
- allow work to be saved, printed out or adapted for future use
- can increase pupil motivation
- are good for class demonstrations
- can help teachers explain difficult concepts
- have lots of tools for editing and manipulating text and graphics
- allow pupils to use touch to operate the board and use their own handwriting to input data or information
- have lots of useful tools, such as highlighters, different coloured pens and erasers
- can be enhanced by all the extra software available
- can be fun to use!

Using an interactive whiteboard

○ If the board is portable, check that all the necessary components are in place, such as cables. Be very careful when setting up, making sure that there are no trailing cables for people to trip over.

○ Make sure it is installed correctly. Can all the pupils see the screen from their seats? Is the height appropriate for the size of your pupils – it shouldn't be set at adult height!

○ An interactive whiteboard is not simply a replacement for a blackboard – it's a sophisticated piece of equipment. You should receive some training on how to use it before deploying it in your classroom.

○ Practise using the tools and also make sure that you are familiar with the software.

○ Start off slowly – use just a few tools with the class and then add more as you and your pupils gain confidence.

○ Don't forget that you can display a wide range of media on your whiteboard.

○ Make sure that you have good-quality, wall-mounted speakers for sound and music.

○ Remember, brainstorming activities are very popular and encourage children to get involved with their learning.

Data projectors

Although prices of interactive whiteboards are falling, they are still expensive. A cheaper alternative is a data projector and screen.

Why use a data projector?

○ They cost less, which means that a school could invest in several or more of them, thus opening up the facility to more teachers.
○ They are portable, so they can be used around the school.
○ They can be used with a laptop or tablet PC and the projector and computer can be linked by a wireless connection.
○ They can be used with a normal white screen.
○ They can also be used as video projectors.

The disadvantages

○ The display isn't interactive.
○ Annotations can't be saved.
○ It may be harder to find appropriate third-party software.
○ Security can be an issue, as these are very popular products with thieves.

Going Online

LIST 44   Making the most of the Internet

The rise of the Internet means that literally a whole new world can come into the classroom and there are many fantastic opportunities for learning and communicating. It also means that learning can take place almost anywhere and anytime.

The Internet offers you and your school:

- access to vast amounts of content and information
- access to experts from around the globe
- the ability to communicate with others anytime and anywhere
- a giant forum for discussing endless topics
- access to museums, galleries and libraries
- the ability to download software and resources
- opportunities to publish your work to the world
- opportunities to showcase your school via your own website
- the chance to strengthen links between home and school
- the chance to strengthen links with your local community
- access to other teachers for sharing ideas and experiences
- distance learning and e-learning, e.g. from home
- contact with other cultures for greater understanding, language development, etc.
- online training courses and professional development activities.

<table>
<tr><td>L I S T
45</td><td></td></tr>
</table>

L I S T 45 — Using the Internet for teaching and learning

The Internet is a terrific resource but don't forget that traditional forms of resources, such as books, videos, TV programmes, radio, newspapers and magazines, still have much to offer.

○ The Internet can provide up-to-the-minute information, unlike a book or a magazine, but even online information goes out of date, so check when a website or page was last updated.

○ Encourage students to seek out several sources and cross-check the information.

○ Remember that many websites and pages contain errors.

○ Make sure that pupils can differentiate between fact and opinion!

○ Warn pupils about the issue of plagiarism and how it is not acceptable to download information and try and pass it off as your own.

○ Also warn them about issues such as copyright and libel.

○ Remind them of your school's acceptable use policy and how to use the Internet safely (see List 31 Developing a school policy).

○ If you want students to look at a specific website, make sure you examine it thoroughly for content. Also check the links.

○ Many websites are ephemeral so, if you can, download and cache (store) a really useful website resource. Useful web pages should also be printed out and filed.

LIST 46 Resources for online work

The Internet connects computers to an incredible wealth of information and a means of communicating to others around the world. If you or your students are going online, the following tools will make it easier – and safer – to explore the Internet:

- ❍ Web browser – used for exploring the Internet and is launched from the computer desktop by clicking on it.
- ❍ Search engines – make it easier to find things on the Internet.
- ❍ File compressors – make files smaller and thus quicker to download and easier to store.
- ❍ Filters – help keep out unwanted web content.
- ❍ Firewalls – control the data traffic between your computer or network and the Internet.
- ❍ Plug-ins – make it possible to use extra features, such as Flash animations, and play sound and video files.
- ❍ Graphics converters – enable you to convert one file format to another.

Useful features on a web browser

Web browsers have many features that can make exploring the Internet quicker, easier and safer.

○ The tool bar running across the top of the screen has lots of handy features.

○ You don't have to type in the full Internet address. Forget http:// if it's followed by a www. In most cases you won't even need to type in the www prefix.

○ Bookmarks or favourites lists let you store the web address of a really good website you might want to revisit.

○ The home page is the default page that the browser opens up on. This can be changed, although your school network manager has probably blocked this option. However, you can change it on your home PC by going to the Internet options page on your browser.

○ The history feature stores the addresses of all the websites you've visited over a pre-set time and is handy if you've lost the address of a website you previously visited.

○ If a web page is taking ages to load up, click the refresh button.

○ If your web browser has a pop-up blocker, activate it.

○ Don't forget you can customize the browser, for example, by increasing the text size, changing the font style, ignoring certain colours, switching on or off sound, video, graphics and animation on web pages (see List 100 Finding the right buttons).

LIST 48

Why use a web cache?

A web cache is a server that sits between your school's network and the Internet and stores web content, such as pages and graphics. Once set-up, teachers can use an on-screen menu to download and store online content, which can be accessed off-line. There are a number of reasons for using one in schools.

- As a means of using your school's Internet connection more efficiently. Instead of a whole group of pupils trying to access the Internet at the same time, many of them could get their web content from the web cache and so free up bandwidth.
- As a way of speeding up access to web content. Some web content, such as large video files, can take a long time to download from the Internet, but arrive on the desktop computer much faster from a cache.
- As a reliable source of web content. Internet connections can go down and web servers can crash, but if your web content is stored on a web cache, it is immune from these problems.
- As a web filter ensuring that students only use the content you want them to have.
- As a means of focusing web research on relevant content.

LIST 49 Using the Internet in a lesson

○ Make sure that there is a good reason for going online and that the students have clear, focused tasks.

○ Things to check – are the computers and Internet connection booked? Are there enough computers? Do the students have the skills to carry out the online tasks? Are the websites and links still live and is the content still relevant?

○ Mix and match online and off-line work. This also helps if there is a shortage of classroom computers and Internet connections.

○ If possible, use a web cache to store websites and pages that are going to be used extensively. A web cache is also a good insurance in case the Internet connection goes down.

○ Do you want the pupils to explore the Internet or go to pre-defined websites?

○ What outcomes are you expecting from the work, for example, improved ICT skills, a presentation or written work?

LIST 50   E-learning

There's a lot of talk about e-learning (electronic learning) and over
the years, more and more secondary schools are set to go down this
route, because of the amazing flexibility it offers. E-learning consists
of a number of components:

○ online access so that learning can take place anywhere and
anytime
○ communication systems like email, chat and messaging
○ online courses and content
○ online support
○ online assessment and tracking.

Some schools are packaging all these components into virtual
learning environments (VLEs), virtual learning and teaching
environments (VLTEs) or managed learning environments (MLEs).
These come under the umbrella term learning platforms.

Benefits of e-learning

E-learning can be used by pupils of all ages, provided they have online access away from school. At present, it tends to be used by older secondary school students, especially for examination work, but its use is expected to expand to other age groups over the years, as there are so many benefits to this type of learning.

- Students and teachers are not tied to the classroom or the school hours.
- Teachers can create lessons and content and post it online for students to access wherever and whenever.
- Students can store their work and resources online for easy access.
- Students and teachers can contact each other via email, chat, messaging, video conferencing or voice over the Internet.
- Students can submit work electronically.
- Teachers can track and assess students online.
- Students can get a personalized learning experience, with content and teaching and learning strategies that suit their individual needs and strengths.
- Teachers can collect and package a vast array of online content and resources.

Bridging the digital divide

E-learning offers great potential, but it pre-supposes that all students have a computer and Internet connection at home. In fact, large numbers do not and schools need to tackle this. Here are some possible solutions.

○ Setting up a computer loans system.
○ Offering a computer leasing service.
○ Fundraising to purchase more computers.
○ Running after-school and lunchtime computer clubs.
○ Opening a community ICT centre.
○ Contacting a computer recycling organisation such as Free Computers for Education (www.free-computers.org) or Recycle IT! (www.recycle-it.ltd.uk).
○ Joining the E-Learning Foundation, a charity set up to increase access to ICT in education (www.e-learningfoundation.com).
○ Forming links with local businesses for sponsorship or taking donations of old computers.

LIST 53 Tips for video conferencing

Video conferencing is a great way of communicating with others. As you can both see and hear the person (or group) you're communicating with, it adds a new dimension to teaching and learning. Video conferencing doesn't require lots of expensive equipment – a cheap webcam, broadband connection and some software will get your school up and running.

○ Talk to your LEA or regional broadband consortium for advice on video conferencing.

○ Decide how you want to use video conferencing – on a one-to-one or large-group basis?

○ A good connection is more important than lots of fancy kit.

○ A digital projector and whiteboard or an interactive whiteboard are useful when using video conferencing with a large group.

○ Good quality loudspeakers will greatly improve sound quality, particularly on laptop computers.

○ Some school firewalls (which are designed to control Internet traffic) can block video-conferencing systems, so seek advice on getting around this problem.

○ If you're contacting schools abroad, bear in mind that there are time zones. In some cases, you may need to be in school earlier or later than usual in order to connect to another school at a reasonable time for them.

○ Video conferencing works best as part of other forms of online collaboration, such as email or chat, rather than as a stand alone 'special event'.

○ Rather than just having children talking to each other over the video-conferencing link, get them to show each other artefacts, e.g. for a bird project, show different bird seeds or pictures of birds.

Websites for teachers

There are lots of great online resources for teachers, whether you are planning a trip, looking for inspiration or want guidance on how use ICT in the classroom. The following list of general sites is designed for teachers of children of all age ranges:

- 24 Hour Museum (www.24hourmuseum.org.uk) – a guide to over 3,000 museums, galleries and heritage sites
- BBC Education (www.bbc.co.uk/schools) – learning resources
- Becta (www.becta.org.uk) – British Educational Communications and Technology Agency
- BYTEachers (www.byteachers.org.uk) – teaching resources and materials
- Culham (www.culham.ac.uk) – promoting and supporting religious education
- Curriculum Online (www.curriculumonline.gov.uk) – multimedia resources
- Danny Nicholson (www.dannynicholson.co.uk) – teaching resources
- DfES (www.dfes.gov.uk) – Department for Education and Skills
- Edulinks (www.edulinks.co.uk) – lots of educational links
- Edupics (www.edupics.com) – educational colouring pictures
- Eduweb (www.eduweb.com) – online learning activities for art, science and history
- E-School Net (http://eschoolnet.eun.org/ww/en/pub/eschoolnet/index.htm) – European teachers' portal
- European Schoolnet (www.eun.org/portal/index.htm) – European teaching and learning community
- Hot Potatoes (http://web.uvic.ca/hrd/halfbaked/) – for creating games
- ICT Advice (www.ictadvice.org.uk) – Becta ICT advice and guidance
- Learn Trips (www.learntrips.co.uk) – 1,000 venues for school trips across the UK
- Learn.co.uk (www.learn.co.uk) – resources for primary and secondary schools
- Learning and Teaching Scotland (www.ltscotland.org.uk) – advice and resources

- Living Paintings (www.livingpaintings.org) – artworks for visually impaired children
- National Curriculum Online (www.nc.uk.net) – programmes of study and attainment targets
- National Grid for Learning (www.ngfl.gov.uk) – resources and web links
- NCSL (www.ncsl.org.uk) – National College for School Leadership
- Ofsted (www.ofsted.gov.uk)
- Primary Resources (www.primaryresources.co.uk) – lesson plans, activity ideas and resources
- School Zone (www.schoolzone.co.uk) – packed with resources
- Standards website (www.standards.dfes.gov.uk) – DfES site
- Superhighway Safety (http://safety.ngfl.gov.uk/) – Internet safety advice
- Teacher Line (www.teacherline.org.uk) – teacher support network
- Teacher Network (www.theteachernet.co.uk) – teacher support network
- TeacherNet (www.teachernet.gov.uk) – covers all aspects of teaching
- Teachers' TV (www.teacherstv.org.uk) – information and resources featured on the TV channel
- Teaching Ideas (www.teachingideas.co.uk) – for primary teachers
- TEEM (www.teem.org.uk) – teachers evaluating multimedia
- Time to Teach (www.timetoteach.co.uk) – tons of free resources
- *The Times Educational Supplement* (www.tes.co.uk)
- Top Marks (www.topmarks.co.uk) – lots of resources for teachers, students and parents
- Training and Development Agency for Schools (www.tda.gov.uk) – information on all aspects of teaching
- Virtual Teacher Centre (www.vtc.ngfl.gov.uk) – free education information
- World Class (www.bbc.co.uk/worldclass) – for linking your school with others.

LIST 55 Online fun for pupils

You'll find many educational sites aimed at pupils and most of them include an element of fun in the form of games, puzzles or brainteasers. Here is a selection of sites for pupils of all ages.

- At School (www.atschool.co.uk) – a guide for using the Internet and its resources for nursery and primary school-age children
- BBC Revision (www.bbc.co.uk/schools/revision) – a revision guide for ages 7–16
- Book Box (www.channel4.com/learning/microsites/B/bookbox/home.htm) – information about favourite authors and their books
- ChildLine (www.childline.org.uk) – information about the free helpline for young people
- Creating Music.com (www.creatingmusic.com) – showing children how to compose music and play music games and puzzles
- Crucial Crew (www.crucial-crew.org) – workshops giving life-saving safety messages for children aged 8–11
- Don't Suffer in Silence (www.dfes.gov.uk/bullying) – government
- anti-bullying site
- Fabulous Fiction (www.fabfiction.moonfruit.com) – designed to get young people into reading
- First Light (www.firstlightmovies.com) – for young filmmakers
- Fizzy Funny Fuzzy.com (www.fizzyfunnyfuzzy.com) – fun poetry
- Free Foto (www.freefoto.com) – tens of thousands of free images for non-commercial use
- Goldstar Café (www.goldstarcafe.net) – international online community for 11–14-year-olds
- GridClub (www.gridclub.com) – hundreds of games for 7–12-year-olds
- GridClub Superclubs (http://clubs.gridclub.com) – primary school-age students' online community
- Homework High – (www.channel4.com/learning/microsites/H/homeworkhigh) – help with homework
- How Stuff Works (www.howstuffworks.com) – packed with information on science, money, computers, health, etc.

- Jig Zone (www.jigzone.com) – online jigsaw puzzles
- LifeBytes (www.lifebytes.gov.uk) – health facts for 11–14-year-olds
- Pupil Vision (www.pupilvision.com) – for secondary-age geography students
- Think.com (www.think.com) – online educational community
- Word Search Factory (www.kidsdomain.com/down/pc/wordsearchfactory.html) – helps you to create printable word searches!

Websites for parents

Don't forget that many parents will be looking for advice, information and guidance and will be grateful if you can point them towards websites that could be useful. Many of these sites also contain links for further advice.

- Advisory Centre for Education (www.ace-ed.org.uk) – information on all aspects of state education
- Bully Free Zone (www.bullyfreezone.co.uk) – anti-bullying advice
- Dyslexia Institute (www.dyslexia-inst.org.uk) – all aspects of dyslexia
- National Parent Partnership Network (www.parentpartnership.org.uk) – special educational needs information
- Parental Involvement (www.standards.dfes.gov.uk/ parentalinvolvement) – school/parent partnership
- Parents Centre (www.dfes.gov.uk/parents) – government information site for parents
- Parents for Inclusion (www.parentsforinclusion.org) – a network of parents of disabled children
- Parents Information Network (www.pin.org.uk) – ICT advice
- Talk to Frank (www.talktofrank.com) – drugs education
- Talking Point (www.talkingpoint.org.uk) – information on speech, language and communication difficulties.

ICT across the Subjects 7

Making ICT work for English

ICT can be used to develop many skills in English, including reading, writing, speaking and listening. There's also the option of adding multimedia content like pictures and sound to written work. Here are some ideas for activities and the ICT equipment you could use.

○ Digital projector or interactive whiteboard – for presentations, group work, whole-class teaching.

○ Digital camcorder – for recording video which can be used to stimulate discussion or written work.

○ Digital still camera – for taking images that can be imported into a word processor or presentation. As a means of stimulating discussion or a written task, e.g. 'What's happening in this picture?'

○ Tablet PC – for writing stories by hand and putting the text straight into a computer.

○ Laptop PC – why only write in the classroom? A laptop means pupils can write stories, record observations or collaborate in small groups almost anywhere!

○ Portable word processor – far less complicated than a PC, a portable world processor is a good way of introducing children to writing on a computer.

○ Interactive voting system – this allows students to vote from their seat using a small remote control-type handset and registering their views on a large class display. This is a great way of stimulating debate and assessing the general view on a topic or issue.

○ Wireless keyboard and mouse – gives you the freedom to interact with the computer from almost anywhere in the classroom.

○ Scanner – for putting text and images from books, newspapers and magazines into a computer.

- Digital audio recorder – ideal for recording speech and music, such as stories and songs which can be used to inspire written work.
- Webcam – a good way of collaborating with other students in other schools and sharing ideas and experiences.

English: websites

- English Resources – www.newi.ac.uk/englishresources
- Literacy Lessons – www.literacylessons.co.uk
- Poetry Class – www.poetryclass.net
- Teach IT – www.teachit.co.uk/
- Universal Teacher – www.universalteacher.org.uk
- English Biz – www.englishbiz.co.uk
- Spellzone – www.spellzone.com
- Primary Resources – www.primaryresources.co.uk
- English Teaching in the UK – www.english1.org.uk
- Absolute Shakespeare – http://absoluteshakespeare.com
- Novel Guide – www.novelguide.com
- Lord of the Flies – www.gerenser.com/lotf
- Roald Dahl – www.roalddahlfans.com
- Book Box – www.channel4.com/learning/microsites/B/bookbox/
- Kids' Review – www.kidsreview.org.uk/index.asp

Making ICT work for mathematics

Whether you want your students to measure and record, make a presentation to a group or collect data from a variety of sources, ICT can help.

- Data projector or interactive whiteboard – ideal for class presentations, demonstrating concepts and solutions.
- Data logger – pupils can use this to collect data, create graphs on a computer and look for patterns.
- Digital camera – the natural world is full of interesting shapes and patterns, so why not get pupils to record them with a digital camera and then import the images into a computer for some mathematical work?
- Audio recorder – a good way of helping pupils learn how to count.
- Graphics calculator – the latest versions are essentially handheld computers, so pupils can do quite complex mathematics work on these devices.
- Pocket PC or personal digital assistant (PDA) – an ideal device for entering data away from the classroom, such as a traffic survey on a street.
- Control kit – use these for exploring concepts such as time, distance and angle.
- Laptop PC – a laptop means pupils can collect and record data around school or out in the field.
- Tablet PC – some mathematical equations can be tricky to type, but a tablet PC lets pupils compose them with their own handwriting. Tablet PCs are also great for survey work.

Mathematics: websites

- Maths Zone – www.mathszone.co.uk
- Teaching Tables – www.teachingtables.co.uk
- Maths is Fun – www.mathsisfun.com
- Donna Young – http://donnayoung.org/maths
- Primary Resources – www.primaryresources.co.uk/maths
- Skoool – www.skoool.co.uk
- Waldo's Interactive Maths – www.waldomaths.com
- EMaths – www.emaths.co.uk
- MathsNet www.mathsnet.net
- Interactive Maths – www.cut-the-knot.org/content.shtml
- Convert It – www.convert-it.co.uk/ntablemenu.htm
- GCSE Maths Revision – www.mathsrevision.net/gcse/index.php
- Nick's Mathematical Puzzles – www.qbyte.org/puzzles
- Maths File Game Show – www.bbc.co.uk/education/mathsfile/gameswheel.html
- Big Sums – http://ngfl.northumberland.gov.uk/maths/big%20sums/Default.htm

Making ICT work for science

There are lots of ICT tools for measuring and recording all kinds of data and physical phenomena, and portable ICT equipment means your pupils are not tied to carrying out experiments or investigations in the classroom.

○ Data loggers – use sensors to record a wide range of physical phenomena, such as temperature, light and heart rate.

○ Laptop PC – take a laptop on a field trip and record data or access a database. For example, why not put pictures of plants on a laptop and let your pupils use it to identify them?

○ Pocket PC or personal digital assistant (PDA) – these portable computers are ideal for recording data outside the classroom.

○ Control kits – pupils can use these to create all kinds of devices and learn how to control them.

○ Digital camera – these are ideal for taking images, for example, of the local pond, which can be put into a computer or posted online.

○ Digital camcorder – ideal for recording moving video and analysing it. Don't forget, you can import digital camera footage into a PC. Physics experiments or chemical reactions, for example, can be recorded and then analysed on a PC.

○ Digital microscope – these add a new dimension to microscope work, as pupils can view images and store them on a PC.

○ Data projector or interactive whiteboard – presentations, discussions and whole-group exercises can come alive with these devices. Ideal for whole-class demonstrations too.

○ Tablet PC – great for writing out chemical formulae and putting them into a computer.

Science: websites

○ How Stuff Works – www.howstuffworks.com
○ NASA – www.nasa.gov
○ Teaching Ideas – www.teachingideas.co.uk/science
○ BBC Science – www.bbc.co.uk/sn
○ Nature Grid – www.naturegrid.org.uk
○ Planet Science – www.planet-science.com
○ Science Museum – www.nmsi.ac.uk
○ Skoool – www.skoool.co.uk
○ Simply Science – http://users.pipeline.com.au/jpearce/
○ Primary Resources – www.primaryresources.co.uk
○ Yucky Science – http://yucky.kids.discovery.com
○ Info Please – www.infoplease.com
○ Science Active – www.science-active.co.uk
○ The Solar System in Action – www.harmsy.freeuk.com/orrery.html
○ Chemguide – www.chemguide.co.uk

LIST 63   Making ICT work for humanities

ICT has opened up new horizons for humanities teaching, especially when it comes to recording data, collecting information and presenting your results.

○ Digital camera – why not get your pupils to record images when doing field work and use them in their reports?

○ Digital camcorder – observations can be recorded with moving pictures and sound and the video footage can be played back in the classroom.

○ Data logger – these are great for recording data, such as weather information.

○ Tablet PC – easier to use than a laptop when doing field work, as they are smaller and users can record data using handwriting.

○ Laptop PC – there's no need for pupils to be stuck in a classroom when using ICT. Many laptops are lightweight and ideal for taking outside.

○ Pocket PC or personal digital assistant (PDA) – these pocket-sized devices are useful for groups recording data out in the field.

○ Data projector or interactive whiteboard – ideal for large group presentations and demonstrations.

○ Large-screen video display – use this for video presentations, such as camcorder recordings made by the pupils.

○ Audio recorder – use these for recording voice memos and testimonies.

Humanities: websites

- Atlapedia www.atlapedia.com
- Earthquakes for Kids – http://earthquake.usgs.gov/4kids
- Geographical Association – www.geography.org.uk
- GeoResources – www.georesources.co.uk
- Get Mapping – www.getmapping.com
- Map Zone – www.mapzone.co.uk
- Internet Geography – www.geography.learnontheinternet.co.uk
- Royal Geographical Society – www.rgs.org
- For Geography Teachers – http://members.aol.com/bowermanb/teach.html
- Teaching Geography – http://easyweb.easynet.co.uk/-rwilliams/
- 24 Hour Museum – www.24hourmuseum.org.uk
- Seven Wonders of the Ancient World – http://ce.eng.usf.edu/pharos/wonders/
- Lore and Saga – www.lore-and-saga.co.uk
- Anne Frank – www.annefrank.eril.net
- Imperial War Museum – www.iwm.org.uk
- Learning Curve – www.learningcurve.gov.uk
- School History – www.schoolhistory.co.uk
- Learn History – www.learnhistory.org.uk
- Think History – www.thinkhistory.btinternet.co.uk

LIST 65 Making ICT work for modern foreign languages

Learning a foreign language can be brought to life with ICT, allowing pupils to record and replay speech on a PC, view multimedia materials and even communicate with people in other countries via the Internet.

○ Digital projector or interactive whiteboard – use these for whole-class presentations by yourself or your students.

○ Audio recorder – these can be used for speech recordings, and digital recorder sound files are easy to transfer to a computer for listening and analysis.

○ Microphone – you don't have to have a tape recorder as many PCs will let you record directly onto the hard drive. Note that you'll need audio recording software to use this facility.

○ Headphones – use these for private listening on a PC.

○ Digital camera – get pupils to take digital images of everyday objects, transfer them to a PC and use them for language work.

○ Digital camcorder – for recording moving video, for example, a dialogue between two students or teacher and student.

○ Scanner – ideal for importing text and pictures from newspapers and magazines into a computer.

○ Video-conferencing system – for communicating across the Internet. A great way of keeping in touch with schools from other countries.

○ Satellite TV system – for foreign language programmes, such as those on news and current affairs.

○ Tablet PC – why not get your students to make a shopping list or some other list and instead of typing it, use their handwriting to enter data into a computer?

LIST 66 Modern foreign languages: websites

- French search engines – www.google.fr and http://fr.yahoo.com
- German search engines – www.google.de and http://de.yahoo.com
- Spanish search engines – www.google.es and http://es.yahoo.com
- Free Translation – www.freetranslation.com
- French Teacher – www.frenchteacher.net
- French Tutorial – www.frenchtutorial.com
- Lingua Central – www.linguacentral.co.uk
- Teach Spanish – www.teachspanish.com
- ¡Oye! – http://oye.languageskills.co.uk/
- Gut! – http://gut.languageskills.co.uk
- The Ashcombe School website – www.ashcombe.surrey.sch.uk
- LinguaScope – www.linguascope.com
- Liberation newspaper – www.liberation.fr
- Asterix – www.asterix.tm.fr
- BBC Talk – www.bbclanguages.com/talk
- Royalty Free Clip Art for Flash Cards – http://tell.fll.purdue.edu/JapanProj//FLClipart
- SchoolNet Global – www.schoolnetglobal.com
- The Big Project – www.thebigproject.co.uk/news

LIST 67 Making ICT work for art and design

ICT isn't designed to replace the traditional skills of using pencil, paint and paper, but it does offer new and exciting ways for pupils to express their creativity.

○ Digital camera – use for taking still images for class projects, importing pictures into a paint package or simply for inspiration!

○ Scanner – for importing text or graphics into a computer.

○ Tablet PC – for putting freehand drawings, sketches and designs into a computer.

○ Visualizer – instead of displaying flat two-dimensional images, you can use this to show solid objects on a screen for stimulating ideas or for drawing exercises.

○ Digital projector or interactive whiteboard – a great way of showing a pupil's work to the class and also for class presentations and demonstrations.

○ Graphics tablet – use this to get your students to put their hand-drawn sketches directly into a computer.

○ Audio recorder – for recording sounds for inspiration.

○ Sensors – you can use these in food technology work, e.g. for measuring temperature.

Art and design: websites

- Access Art – www.accessart.org.uk
- Art Teaching – www.artteaching.co.uk
- African and Asian Visual Art Archive – www.uel.ac.uk/aavaa/will.html
- Artscape – www.artscape.org.uk
- Tate – www.tate.org.uk
- Museum of Modern Art – www.moma.org
- William Morris Gallery – www.lbwf.gov.uk/wmg/home.htm
- The National Portrait Gallery – www.npg.org.uk
- Textiles Museum of Canada – www.museumfortextiles.on.ca
- CAD in Schools – www.cadinschools.org
- DATA (Design and Technology Association) – www.data.org.uk
- D&T Online – www.dtonline.org
- Design Council – www.designcouncil.org.uk
- Food Forum – www.foodforum.org.uk
- Textiles Online – www.e4s.org.uk/
- Technology Student – www.technologystudent.com

LIST 69   Making ICT work for music

ICT can be used for creating music, recording and manipulating sound and much more. It encourages pupils to experiment and can help them learn the fundamentals of music.

○ Audio recorders – ideal for recording sounds and music and playing them back to pupils.
○ MIDI (Musical Instrument Digital Interface) electronic keyboard – connect this to a computer and let your pupils experiment with sounds and composition.
○ Microphones – you can use these for recording sound into a computer. Try and use a good quality microphone if you can.
○ Headphones – pupils can use these for private listening.
○ Digital metronome – use these for timekeeping exercises.
○ Musical instruments – try and expose pupils to a mix of acoustic and electronic instruments and compare the differences both in terms of sound and function.
○ Desktop or laptop computer with sound card – use this for playing music files which the pupils have created.
○ External speakers – you'll get much better sound quality if you plug a pair of these in your computer, rather than using the PC's built-in speaker.
○ Digital projector or interactive whiteboard – ideal for large group presentations and demonstrations.
○ DJ mixer – a great tool for letting pupils have fun and learn about making music! These programs have lots of mixing and sampling features.
○ Digital tuner – these are easier to use and more accurate when tuning instruments.
○ CD burner – when your pupils have created their musical masterpiece, why not burn them a copy to play to their parents at home?
○ Audio mixer – experimenting with sound is great fun and highly educational, so use an audio mixer to teach children about the art of blending sounds.
○ Digital camcorder – pupils can learn a lot by watching their performances.
○ CD deck (CD-ROM drive in a PC will do) – use this for playing music CDs.

Music: websites

- Creating Music – www.creatingmusic.com
- ICT and Music (primary school) –
  www.hitchams.suffolk.sch.uk/ictmusic/index.htm
- Free music software for downloading – www.metronimo.com/uk
- Free karaoke player – www.vanbasco.com
- Music glossary – www.naxos.com/mgloss.htm
- Classical Net – www.classical.net/music
- Music scores – www.music-scores.com
- Music for Youth – www.mfy.org.uk
- Jazz sheet music – www.jazzuk.demon.co.uk
- Sheet music – www.halleonard.com
- Music at School – www.musicatschool.co.uk
- Online music encyclopaedia – http://library.thinkquest.org/
  10400/html/index.html
- Instrument jokes (have some fun!) – www.mit.edu/people/jcb/
  jokes
- The Music Land – www.themusicland.co.uk
- Music Teachers – www.musicteachers.co.uk

LIST 71 Making ICT work for PE

There are many opportunities for using ICT in PE, from recording data during exercise to analysing performances on a computer or interactive whiteboard.

○ Digital camcorder – use for recording performances and then analysing technique by looking at the recording in slow motion or frame-by-frame.
○ Digital camera – use to record still images for studying posture or technique.
○ Music player – good for playing music during dance lessons.
○ Digital projector or interactive whiteboard – use for large group presentations and demonstrations.
○ Laptop, tablet PC or pocket PC – these portable devices are ideal for recording data out in the field, such as lap times or speed.
○ Data logger – great for seeing how exercise affects the body. Use these for recording pupil data, such as heart rate, temperature and breathing.
○ Digital stopwatch – provides accurate recording of pupil performances.
○ CD-ROM/DVD-ROM drive – there are lots of useful software packages in this subject area and these are ideal for playing them on.

- Food Fitness – www.foodfitness.org.uk
- British Heart Foundation – www.bhf.org.uk
- Sport England – www.sportengland.com
- QCA PE & School Sports – www.qca.org.uk/pess
- BBC Bitesize PE – www.bbc.co.uk/schools/gcsebitesize/pe
- Fun and Fitness – www.fun-and-fitness.com
- Physical Education Association – www.pea.co.uk
- Virtual Sports Injury Clinic – www.sportsinjuryclinic.net
- Teaching Ideas: PE – www.teachingideas.co.uk/pe/contents.htm
- Frank and Mike's Physical Education Page – www.geocities.com/sissio/physical_education.html
- PE Central – www.pecentral.org
- Kidnetic – www.kidnetic.com
- History of Football – www.soccer.mistral.co.uk
- BBC Health – www.bbc.co.uk/health
- Fitness Jumpsite – http://primusweb.com/fitnesspartner

Making ICT work for RE

Religious education (RE) presentations can be brought to life with ICT, and it also offers many ways of recording events and presenting them on a computer or to a whole class.

○ Digital projector or interactive whiteboard – use these for large group presentations or debates.
○ Digital camcorder – good for recording discussions or school visits.
○ Digital camera – pupils can record school visits on their cameras and use them for project work or reports.
○ Audio recorder – for recording discussions, debates or interviews.
○ Video conferencing – a good way of contacting students, teachers and experts in other institutions.
○ Interactive voting system – this allows students to vote from their seat using a small remote control-type handset and registering their views on a large class display. This is a great way of stimulating debate and assessing the general view on a topic or issue.

RE: websites

- Culham Institute – www.culham.ac.uk
- RE Teaching Ideas – www.teachingideas.co.uk/re/contents.htm
- The RE Site – www.reonline.org.uk
- ICTeachers RE – www.icteachers.co.uk/resources/resources_re.htm
- RE ideas for primary schools – www.infant-resources.co.uk/re.htm
- Assemblies – www.assemblies.org.uk
- Christianity – http://library.thinkquest.org/28505/christianity/intro.htm
- Christian Artefacts – www.reonline.org.uk/shells/strath_cafacts.html
- Islam for Children – http://atschool.eduweb.co.uk/carolrb/islam/islamintro.html
- Mosque and Synagogue virtual tours – www.hitchams.suffolk.sch.uk/Resources/page6.html
- Judaism for Children – http://atschool.eduweb.co.uk/carolrb/judaism/judai1.html
- Jewish Artefacts – www.reonline.org.uk/shells/strath_jafacts.html
- Buddhism – http://buddhamind.info
- Hinduism for Schools – www.btinternet.com/~vivekananda/schools.htm

Using ICT for Creativity

Why use digital video in the classroom?

Digital video can bring subjects to life with the aid of moving pictures and sound. In many lessons video is used passively, with pupils watching a video on a TV screen, but ICT gives you and your pupils the opportunity to work actively with the medium, recording, editing, mixing and presenting. Digital video can:

○ stimulate creativity in many ways, whether your students are writing a script or adding special effects to a video clip
○ encourage collaboration and cooperation as groups of students work together on a project
○ motivate pupils to take control over what they create
○ help to raise standards in areas such as literacy and presentational skills
○ use a variety of learning styles – auditory, visual and kinaesthetic
○ be used to create class demonstration materials
○ help to aid understanding, especially with difficult concepts. If a picture is worth a thousand words, a moving picture can be worth hours of explanation
○ be used to create resources that can be used in other lessons or other subject areas
○ help pupils to become more critical about content as they edit and sort materials
○ engage pupils as it more fun to watch a video production produced by yourself or your peers.

Ten good uses of digital video

1 Recording a school concert, drama or dance performance
2 Recording a school field trip or visit
3 Creating a short play
4 Recording a science experiment

5   Helping with sports training – slow motion and frame-by-frame analysis can help pupils develop the right technique
6   Making a video message for another school
7   Making videos for the school website
8   Creating a video diary
9   Recording how a plant grows over a period of time
10 Recording guest speakers and interviews with visitors or members of the local community.

LIST 76 Essential kit for digital video

To use digital video with your pupils there are some vital bits of hardware and software you will require.

- ❍ A digital camcorder. Older analogue camcorders can be used, but their footage needs to be converted to digital and, these days, digital camcorders are so affordable that it makes good sense to purchase one. Digital camcorders come in all shapes and sizes, including ones which record onto tape, DVD discs and hard-disk drives.
- ❍ A powerful PC. This is the workhorse of digital video and is used for storing, editing and manipulating digital video footage.
- ❍ Editing software. This ranges from free software that comes with the computer to commercial software that can cost hundreds of pounds. However, excellent packages can be purchased for less than £50.
- ❍ A DVD burner and software. These are used for putting your footage onto a DVD disc.

LIST 77 Getting a PC for video editing

Computers are great for editing video, but in order to do this, you have to use a PC that is powerful enough and flexible enough. So, check that your computer has:

- a very fast processor chip, as video editing places great demands on the computer
- lots of RAM in order to handle massive video files
- a massive hard drive (preferably two), as even a minute of high-quality video uses lots of storage space. You might want to consider a large external hard drive
- a high-quality graphics card with lots of memory
- a Firewire connection, which is used to transfer digital footage from the camcorder to the computer
- a DVD burner for transferring footage to disc
- a high resolution display monitor
- speakers for playing back sound
- lots of connecting ports for audio mixers, recorders, microphone, headphones, etc.

Tips for using a camcorder

○ Make sure that batteries are fully charged before you start shooting. Also consider having a spare battery to hand if you're using the camcorder away from school.

○ Use a tripod to prevent camera shake. Most tripods fold away easily and so are highly portable.

○ Check that the Firewire connection is compatible with your computer – there are variations around and you may need a special lead or adapter.

○ Automatic features have made camcorders very easy to use, but try and avoid using the auto-focus feature, as this can drift out of focus under certain shooting conditions. It also uses battery power. Manual control gives you better results.

○ Always record with the highest picture quality, so avoid settings that extend recording time, such as long play, at the expense of picture quality.

○ Avoid using the digital zoom as this reduces picture quality.

○ Make sure that the students know how to frame a shot, how to avoid shooting for longer than is necessary and why they should use the zoom lens sparingly.

○ Use an external microphone for better sound recordings.

○ Use the LCD screen display sparingly – just for framing the shot and checking recordings – as it soaks up battery power.

○ Screw a sunlight or neutral density filter to the front of the lens if you can, as this will protect it from scratches but have no effect on the overall images.

○ Keep your camcorder well maintained – clean the lens with a lens cleaning cloth and use a video cleaner on the recording heads occasionally.

LIST 79 Using digital video in lessons

Good planning and preparation are vital when you use digital videos in lessons.

○ Make sure that you have the skills to use the camcorder, editing PC and associated software.

○ Check that there is sufficient hardware and software available for the group.

○ Check that the equipment is in good condition, e.g. are the batteries fully charged?

○ Make sure that your students have the basic skills required to use the camcorder.

○ Ensure the pupils know how to use the editing software.

○ Stress the importance of taking care of the equipment, as it is fragile and expensive.

○ Make sure that the pupils are aware of the importance of preserving battery power, e.g. by avoiding over-long shoots or switching off the LCD display when not required.

○ Be aware of copyright issues if you are planning to use commercially recorded music and show your video to a large audience. There are some good music CDs available that can be used for amateur video productions.

○ Remember, security is an issue, especially if students are moving around with expensive equipment. Count everything in and out and get the students to check that they leave nothing behind when they are out and about.

Creating a video

When you are preparing your students to create a digital video, the key to success is freedom within a tight framework!

○ Make sure pupils know what the aim of the video exercise is, what your expectations are (such as a five-minute video with music), who the audience is and what the time frame is for completion. While you don't want to stifle creativity, it's important that the video work is done with some discipline.

○ Divide the class into small groups and get them to sort out who will be doing what.

○ If shooting is to take place away from school (say the local pond), try and get the group to visit it beforehand so that they can assess the area. This will help with their planning and preparation.

○ A basic script needs to be written. Don't be over ambitious – the idea is not to create a Hollywood movie. Short videos that are tightly scripted, shot and edited work best. They require less time to produce and they won't bore your audience.

○ A shooting script or a storyboard needs to be completed before any footage is shot.

○ The production stage involves shooting the footage. Try and get the pupils to consider unusual angles and imaginative narratives – but make sure the ideas are not too whacky!

○ The post-production stage is where the editing, dubbing and special effects are carried out on a computer.

○ The pupils will then present their finished work. Try and encourage constructive debate and criticism among the group.

○ Take time to reflect on the finished video. Establish what worked well and what didn't, and what could be done differently next time.

LIST 81   Get painting

Computers aren't going to replace pencils, paint and paper, but with paint packages they do offer new ways of expressing pupil's creativity in the classroom. There are many reasons why you should consider using one of these.

- Paint packages encourage experimentation because it's very easy to delete or undo work, without having to start again!
- They can be used to explore things such as colour, texture, patterns, symmetry, shape and space.
- They come with lots of tools, including pencils, paint brushes and various ways of creating many different types of shapes.
- You can create design templates for textile work.
- Many packages include ready-made clip art.
- You can combine a pupil's paper and pencil drawing with the paint package by scanning in hand-drawn images and then using the paint package to colour them.
- Images taken on a digital camera can be imported into a paint package and edited and manipulated.
- Work can be displayed to a class or group via an interactive whiteboard or data projector.
- Work can be printed out in full colour.
- Most packages can be used with a variety of input devices, such as graphics tablets and touch screens, so that children with special educational needs can also use them.
- A lot of computers come with basic paint packages, which are a good starting point.
- Many packages offer different types of 'paper' and surfaces to work on.
- Some packages allow users to create simple animations by combining a series of still images.
- Some packages offer additional features, such as the ability to add your voice to an image or animation.

LIST 82 Making music

Computers and computer software offer new and exciting ways of creating music in the classroom (see List 69 Making ICT work for music). What is more, many packages don't require pupils to be able to read music before they start creating their own compositions. More advanced programs enable students to turn the classroom into a miniature recording studio.

Use ICT in music lessons to:

- teach pupils about the basics of music, such as harmony, rhythm, melody and chord sequences, allowing them to create their own compositions on a computer
- learn how different instruments sound, using software programs rather than live instruments
- create multi-track recordings
- do sound editing and sampling
- learn about musical notation and compose scores
- record musical instruments and then manipulate the sound
- link electronic keyboards, drum machines, sequencers and samplers to a computer using the MIDI (Musical Instrument Digital Instrument) standard
- encourage singing with the aid of karaoke machines
- access the wealth of music resources found on the Internet (see List 70 Music: websites).
- create music, record it on a computer and then burn it onto a CD disc.

Planning a multimedia presentation

Multimedia presentations are a great way of reinforcing a concept or topic and require the use of many skills, from literacy to good organization. Many computers have programs like PowerPoint pre-installed, although there are commercial offerings with more features. Multimedia presentations give pupils the opportunity to work with text, images, sound and animation and create slide presentations that can be shown on a computer or via an interactive whiteboard or data projector.

○ Show the class examples of multimedia presentations created by children of a similar age (these can be downloaded from school sites on the Internet). Get your pupils to examine them critically, looking, for example, at what works well, whether the colours clash and if the screens contain too much information.

○ Demonstrate the software they'll be using to create their presentations, highlighting the features and ensuring they know how to use the basic tools, such as how to link pages together.

○ Give the class clear instructions on what you expect from their presentations in terms of content, for example, the approximate number of slides they should aim to create.

○ Arrange your class into small groups (of say, two or three pupils) and get them to write a storyboard or plan of their presentation.

○ Allow them to gather everything they will need for their presentations, using a digital camera to take images, a paint package for drawing or an audio recorder for sound recording.

○ Allow the pupils adequate time to put together their presentations.

○ Get the pupils to introduce their presentations to the class and then run them.

○ Encourage constructive criticism and debate after each presentation.

Creative writing

When it comes to creative writing, computers can help to inspire, enhance and improve the quality of the work produced by pupils. From importing clip art to illustrate a poem, to creating a school newsletter or spellchecking an essay, there are many applications which will help pupils with their writing skills and presentation.

- Word processors and desktop publishing packages allow users to undo, delete, cut and paste and change the font style and colour of the text. Children can experiment, revise and review and make alterations quickly and easily.
- There are many computer-based games, activities and puzzles that can be used to help develop writing skills.
- Talking word processors can help pupils with special educational needs.
- Predictive word processors, which present users with a menu of words to select, can help pupils who have difficulty in typing.
- Images can be imported into text. There is plenty of free clip art and images on the Internet.
- All types of written works can easily be created on a computer, such as newspapers, brochures, books and plays.
- Spellcheckers and grammar checkers are useful for correcting work, but note that they are not infallible!
- Pupils can work together around a computer on collaborative projects.
- Pupils with poor handwriting or motor skills can produce work that looks neat and well presented.
- Work can be printed out, burnt on to a disk or published on the Internet.
- There are countless text resources on the Internet for pupils to explore and examine.

Communication

9

LIST 85   Email in schools

Communication tools such as email and chat have broken down the barriers of time and distance and provided low-cost forms of communication that are within the reach of millions of people. No surprise that schools have taken to electronic forms of communication like ducks to water. Here are some possible uses of email in school.

For pupils:

○ contacting their teacher from home
○ sending essays or projects to their teacher from home
○ contacting pupils from other schools, which may be on a different continent. Many pupils have 'electronic penfriends'.

For teachers:

○ contacting other teachers
○ contacting parents and pupils
○ contacting institutions, such as museums and galleries
○ contacting hotels, field centres and other places when planning a field trip or visit.
○ contacting experts.

For schools:

○ contacting the DfES
○ contacting their LEA
○ keeping in touch with educational suppliers
○ contacting examination boards
○ exchanging files.

For parents:

○ contacting teachers from home.

LIST 86 Email etiquette

○ Email is a wonderful communication tool but before using it, ask whether it is really necessary to send a message. Just because it's quick and easy to send an email doesn't mean you should!

○ Don't let email take over your life – it's important to maintain face-to-face contact or phone contact with people.

○ Remember that an email is somewhere between a letter and a postcard and is not a completely private form of communication.

○ Don't SHOUT in emails by typing in upper case letters.

○ Never fire off an email message in anger. Pause, reflect and then delete the message.

○ Avoid using offensive, abusive or threatening language.

○ Remember that the laws of libel apply to electronic forms of communication, as well as those on paper.

○ Only send humorous or sarcastic remarks to people you know really well – humour doesn't always travel well in cyberspace.

○ Don't give out personal information, such as full name, address or telephone number, unless you know the person really well.

○ Despite what some people say, grammar and spelling do matter when using electronic forms of communication – misspelt emails do jar. Read and re-read your message before sending, and use grammar and spellcheckers if they're available (but remember that these are not infallible).

○ Be careful when replying to a message that has been sent to a group. If you select the wrong reply format, you could end up sending your reply to the whole group.

○ When sending email to a group of people, use the blind carbon copy (BCC) method. This prevents other people from seeing all the email addresses and thus maintains privacy.

○ Some attachments use very large files, which can take ages to download, even with a high-speed broadband connection, so use this facility sparingly. Before sending a large attachment, it's a good idea to check with the would-be recipient that they are happy to receive it. Try and avoid sending 'joke' attachments, especially images.

Sending and receiving emails

○ Your email address is precious, so keep it as private as possible. Spammers will send you lots of unsolicited email if they get hold of it.

○ If a website requests your email address, try to avoid giving it unless absolutely necessary. It's a good idea to set up an alternative email account for such communications, as this will help to reduce the risk of spam in your personal account.

○ Remember, you can also send images, sound, music, animations and even video via email.

○ When sending attachments, try and use file formats that can be read by many types of computers, such as text files and Jpeg images. If the two computers use different operating systems, such as Apple and PC, compatibility can sometimes be an issue. If you're sending text, you can paste it into the body of the email and this will be readable on any computer.

○ Always use a virus scanner before opening any attachment, even from people you know. Spammers and virus writers can spoof or hijack genuine email names and addresses to conceal their true origins.

○ You can often check where an email message came from before opening it. If you use Microsoft Outlook, for example, right click on the message and then select 'Option' from the pop-up menu. Scroll down the text and you'll find the name of the original sender.

○ Always scan outgoing emails, so you don't send anyone a virus or some other computer nasty.

○ Before sending an email, check and re-check the address. Remember, if it's just one character out, it will not be received. Hitting the 'Reply' box on an email and then writing your message will ensure that you have the correct address.

○ Never, ever reply to spam. It will simply generate more spam.

○ Spam filters can help, but they are not infallible. If you are receiving lots of spam from the same source, complain to your Internet service provider.

○ Keep a copy of the email you've sent in case you have to re-send it – emails can get lost in cyberspace.

○ Back up or print out important emails.

○ Regularly clear out your email inbox and sent box.

LIST 88 Using chat and instant messaging

Chat and instant messaging are to email what the telephone is to the letter – they provide real-time communication. This makes them fantastic tools for collaboration, but there are some useful guidelines to follow.

❍ Try and use chat rooms that have been specially set up for education, such as Grid Club, Grid Superclubs and Gold Star Café (see List 55 Online fun for pupils). These are tightly controlled and monitored.

❍ Pupils should be encouraged to use nicknames rather than their real names and ideally names that are gender neutral.

❍ Pupils should never post personal information on a chat site.

❍ Abusive, offensive or threatening language should not be used.

❍ Remind pupils that not everyone is who they seem on the Internet.

❍ Pupils should never arrange to contact or meet someone they've only met on a chat forum.

❍ If pupils receive an inappropriate message, they should be encouraged to inform someone in authority.

❍ Instant messaging (IM) is private, one-to-one communication rather than within a group, as in the case of chat. The same rules apply and pupils should set up their IM account so they can only receive messages from specific persons. This helps avoid spim – the instant messaging equivalent of spam.

Making a web page

The days when you needed to be a 'techie' to produce a web page are long gone. These days, if you can use a word processor, you can create a web page, thanks to the new generation of web-creation programs. These so-called WISYWYG (what you see is what you get) programs are designed to take the pain out of web-page creation by using simple operations such as dragging and dropping the various elements.

Things to consider

- Keep it simple. Clean, clear pages are better than 'busy' pages cluttered up with lots of text and graphics.
- Use simple fonts and colours.
- Go easy on the amount of text you use – reading text on screen is not the same as reading it on a page.
- Go easy on flash animations, which can take a long time to load – and also irritate people!
- Make sure your text doesn't clash with the background colours.
- Avoid using lots of large graphics as these take ages to load.
- Use special effects like flashing text sparingly – just because you have a feature doesn't mean you have to use it!
- Make it easy to navigate around the page with large buttons and clear instructions.
- Use frames (sub-pages) sparingly as some browsers can have problems with these.
- Make sure that you don't breach copyright by using images or text that is someone else's intellectual property.
- Make sure that your page is accessible by people with special needs, such as those with visual impairments. This means providing text descriptions of images, for example, and making your page friendly for screen readers, which read screen text back to the user.
- Try to avoid making pages that require users to scroll down lots of text. If there's a lot of content, then create an additional page or pages.
- Test and check your web page. Are the spellings correct? Do all the buttons work? Do the links work? Do the animations launch as they should?

LIST 90 **Pupil web pages**

Creating web pages is a great way of getting pupils to present information in a different way. It also calls for many skills, including planning, designing and writing. The pages can be displayed on their PC screen or to the whole group with an interactive whiteboard or data projector. You can even post them on the school intranet or the Internet!

Ideas include:

- my favourite sport
- my favourite music
- my hobby
- my story
- my class project
- a puzzle page
- my neighbourhood
- our local library/gallery/museum
- an issue I feel strongly about
- how something works – my explanation
- how to – my explanation of how to do a specific task (such as look after an animal)
- a school newspaper.

Planning your school website

A school website can be a wonderful showcase for any institution, although great care needs to be taken to ensure that it looks good, is easy to use and communicates the messages you want to convey. Consider some of these points.

○ What is the target audience – staff and students, parents, other schools or the wider community?

○ Will you develop the website in-house or appoint external designers?

○ If it's being developed in-house, who will design it?

○ How will it be maintained and updated?

○ How can you get pupils involved?

○ What content do you want to put on the website?

○ Do you want to give special access to a school intranet for staff and students?

○ Do you want to use features such as podcasting (audio broadcasting) or video downloads?

○ What feedback will you provide for visitors?

○ How do you protect it against hackers?

○ How often will you review its content and function?

○ What domain name will be registered (probably the school's name)?

○ Who will host the website?

○ How will you promote it?

LIST 92 What to include on your school website

- General information – school location and map details.
- A general statement on the school's ethos and expectations.
- Information on school uniform, school hours, term dates, etc.
- Background information – age of students, size of school, size of sixth form (if appropriate).
- Contact details – general telephone number and email address.
- Staff information – headteacher, heads of year, heads of department, special educational needs coordinator.
- School news – awards won, sports results, school concerts.
- Homework schedules.
- Details of school policies, e.g. on bullying, Internet use.
- School reports, such as details about a recent school trip or visit.
- Learning resources or links to resources.
- Information on feeder schools or partner schools.
- Examples of pupils' work.
- Fundraising activities and details of the parent-teacher association, if your school has one.

Designing the website

It's always a good idea to check out other school websites both for inspiration and a warning of what not to do!

○ Keep it simple – don't try to run before you can walk. Start with the basics and then elaborate as the website develops.

○ Don't create an introduction page with a flash animation as this annoys many people who simply want to get to your website.

○ Get the pupils involved – give them a feeling that they share ownership of the website.

○ Go for a clean, clear page design.

○ Keep the number of fonts you use down.

○ Make sure your website is accessible to those with physical disabilities – this is a legal requirement.

○ Photographs can enhance a website but if you use pupils, get their parents' or carers' permission first.

○ Make sure none of the content breaches anyone's copyright. If in doubt, leave it out!

○ If you're using multimedia that requires users to have special plug-ins on their computer, such as Adobe's PDF files or Macromedia's Flash animation, include links for downloading them.

○ Keep the website navigation as simple and as clear as possible. Always provide a back button and a home-page button.

○ Your website will be read by a wide audience, so make sure the language is clear and unambiguous.

○ Before going live, check your website thoroughly – make sure all links, buttons and menus work as they should. Check all spellings!

○ Provide a feedback form or email address to the web manager, so that any faults can be reported.

○ Make sure that there is scope for your website to grow and develop.

○ Remember, a website is not like a page in a book. It's an organic medium that needs to evolve, so regular updates, revisions and reviews are essential.

L I S T 94 School website security

○ Always get parental permission before putting any images of pupils online.

○ Where possible, use group shots rather than images of individuals.

○ Never give a pupil's full name.

○ Never release personal information about staff or pupils, such as addresses, phone numbers or email addresses.

○ Check that you do not use copyrighted material.

○ Ensure that any links do not take visitors to unsavoury or inappropriate websites or pages.

○ Avoid providing tools, such as search engines, that could give users access to inappropriate sites or content.

○ Ensure that your Internet service provider offers good protection against denial-of-service attacks, where hackers bombard your school server with messages that overload it with data and cause it to malfunction.

○ Use an effective firewall to make sure that your school website server cannot be hijacked and used to send spam emails.

LIST 95 Developing your school intranet

Whereas the Internet is a public medium, intranets are private networks, so-called because they're based on Internet technology (they're accessed via a standard web browser). You need to think carefully about how you will use your intranet.

○ Is the intranet for staff only or staff and students or staff, students and parents?
○ Would it be better to have restricted areas for staff access or a separate intranet altogether?
○ Will it be accessible both in school and at home?
○ Who will manage and maintain it?
○ How will it be kept secure? How will passwords be managed?
○ What content will be provided for teachers, e.g. the school calendar, continuous professional development resources and links, staff meeting schedules?
○ What content will be provided for students, e.g. the homework diary, examination timetables, learning resources?
○ What content will be provided for parents, e.g. dates for parents' meetings, homework diaries, pupil test results, pupil attendance details? Bear in mind that some of this data will come under the Data Protection Act, so consider how access will be provided.

Keeping on Top of ICT | 10

LIST 96   Extending the life of your PC

You might think that you need to replace your PC every few years to keep up to date, but that isn't always the case. Here are some things you can do to extend the life of your computer.

- ○ If you're running out of hard-disk space, you can purchase an external hard drive and connect that to your PC. The extra hard drive can also be used for backing up data.
- ○ If your computer doesn't have a DVD writer, you can buy an external one and link it to your PC.
- ○ If you need extra USB sockets, purchase a USB hub, which lets you connect multiple numbers of USB devices to a PC.
- ○ Check manufacturers' websites to see if they have updated the driver software (which lets your computer communicate with devices like the DVD-ROM drive). The latest drivers often make your computer work better and are simply downloaded and installed.
- ○ If your computer is more than a few years old, consider adding more random access memory (RAM) as this will help it run much faster.
- ○ If a new or improved operating system comes along, you may be able to upgrade to it, but before doing so, check that your computer is powerful enough to run it, e.g. you may need to add extra RAM or hard-disk space.

LIST 97 Maintaining your software

○ Make sure your computer is compatible with the software you want to run and that it has sufficient processor power, RAM and hard-disk space. Software comes with a list of minimum and recommended specifications.

○ If you're using Microsoft Windows, check the Windows update website for the latest releases. Go to http:// update.microsoft.com/windowsupdate.

○ Set your computer to receive security updates automatically.

○ Regularly update any anti-virus and anti-spyware software. If possible, set your computer to receive automatic updates.

○ Check whether the software manufacturer has released any patches (which are designed to fix bugs) and if so, download them.

Keeping up to speed with ICT

The ICT world is a fast-moving one and so it's important to keep on top of your ICT skills. This means continuous professional development.

○ Your school should be able to offer training, either in-house or external courses.

○ Your head of department or the person responsible for ICT should be able to advise you on what training is available and when.

○ Check online teacher forums for support and guidance – there's a thriving online community out there. Becta's website is packed with advice (www.becta.org.uk) as are TeacherNet (www.teachernet.gov.uk) and the Virtual Teacher Centre (www.vtc.ngfl.gov.uk).

○ Educational technology journals and supplements are a good source of ICT news and information.

○ Before attending a training course, find out exactly what you are getting for your time and money.

○ The best training courses offer a mix of presentations and hands-on activities.

○ At the end of a training course, try and complete the feedback form as it will help future teachers attending the course.

LIST 99 What to customize on your computer

Why not personalize your computer so that it suits you best and not the person who designed the machine or program? Here are some things you can do.

○ The desktop – change the size of the icons, screen background, colour and design (even add your own picture!).
○ The web browser – change the size and colour of the fonts and choose your preferred home page.
○ Tool bars run along the top and bottom of the screen and contain various tools. You can modify these by adding or removing tools.
○ Use keyboard shortcuts to cut down on the typing.
○ Search engines – you can modify the content you see on the home page.
○ Software – there are often ways of adapting a software package to suit your needs.

LIST 100   Finding the right buttons

Here are some quick, easy ways to get your Windows PC doing some of the things you want it to do!

○ To change the settings on your web browser (such as the home page or clear the web cache), put your mouse pointer over the web browser icon and right click. This brings up a pop-up menu. Select 'Properties' and you'll be taken to the browser settings.

○ To see how much space is left on your hard drive, go to the 'My Computer' icon and double click on it. Select the hard drive you want information about and then right click on it. From the menu select 'Properties' and you'll see a pie chart display which gives a figure for the available free space.

○ The control panel lets you make a variety of changes to your PC, such as changing the monitor display, adjusting the sound level and setting the clock. Go to the 'My Computer' icon and double click on it. On the left-hand side is a menu which includes 'Other Places'. You'll find a listing for the control panel here. Double click to open it. Before making any changes to the control panel, make a note of the setting, so if you make a mistake you can go back to the original setting.

○ If your computer crashes you can use the system restore facility. Go to the program menu, select 'Accessories' from the menu list, then select 'System Tools' and 'System Restore' will appear in this menu list.

○ If you've accidentally deleted a document or file, all is not lost. Go to the 'Recycle Bin' icon and double click on it. This will reveal the contents and your file should be there. Select the file you want and right click on it. You'll be given the option to 'Restore' it. Click and it will return to its original location.

○ If you're word processing and you accidentally delete a passage, or cut the wrong block of text, before doing anything else, go to the 'Edit' menu at the top of the screen and click on it. Select 'Undo Typing' and your text will be returned to its original state.

Why computers won't replace teachers

ICT is a means to an end and despite what you might hear, will never replace teachers at the heart of the classroom. Here are a few reasons why.

○ Human interaction is important to all of us – the smile, nod of encouragement, the quiet word of advice can make all the difference.

○ Humans are more flexible and adaptable than computers. We can change and modify our tactics very quickly. If a computer can't compute, it won't!

○ Computers may cause a teacher's role to change at times, for example from an expert to a facilitator, but the teacher remains at the centre of things in the classroom.

○ Even when pupils are learning online, they need to have regular contact with other people. In the jargon, F2F (face-to-face) contact matters.

○ Teachers don't crash – although they do have their moments!